Frank S. Child

South Dakota

Resources - People - Statehood

Frank S. Child

South Dakota
Resources - People - Statehood

ISBN/EAN: 9783744761932

Printed in Europe, USA, Canada, Australia, Japan

Cover: Foto ©Andreas Hilbeck / pixelio.de

More available books at **www.hansebooks.com**

SOUTH DAKOTA:

Resources— People—Statehood.

THE GLEANINGS OF A JOURNEY THROUGH

THE TERRITORY

—BY—

FRANK S. CHILD.

NEW YORK:

THE BAKER & TAYLOR COMPANY.

MDCCCLXXXVIII.

CONTENTS.

THE COUNTRY.

We were reading with keen interest speeches and narratives that concerned Dakota. The work or the play of Congress seemed a thing of mockery and humiliation. Then it occurred to us that we turn us Dakota-ward and spy out the land. We would measure for ourselves the worth and promise of the Territory. We would set the words of friends over against the words of foes, and then pronounce upon them by the aid of such knowledge as we could glean through personal investigation. The heralded prosperity of Dakota interested us. The throwing open to settlers a share of the Sioux Reservation interested us. The earnest, persistent struggle for Statehood interested us. So we hastened to the Dakota land.

We found Dakota. It is emphatically a " findable " country. The immensity of its landscape appalled us. The extreme north insists that four hundred and thirty miles shall mark the distance from the extreme south. The east is separated from the west by three hundred and eighty-five miles. The area of Dakota is one hundred and fifty thousand nine hundred and thirty-two square miles, or ninety-six million five hundred and ninety-six thousand four hundred and eighty acres.

B

That means that you can pack all New England, Ohio, New York into Dakota and then take some eight or ten Districts of Columbia and fill in the chinks. When we faced this fact, necessity forced us to restrict our observations to South Dakota. And this task proved too large for us. The Black Hills were not visited and many parts of the land were "done" with unsatisfactory haste.

South Dakota alone is text for endless discourse. It is like putting out to sea, this pressing one's way through the billowy vastness of the illimitable prairies. Gentle undulations break the monotony of the land. Luxuriant grasses, glistening grains—they make their swift and graceful responses as the winds touch them with the impulse of summer. The distant smoke which hovers near the horizon for a time and then dis appears in the cloudless sky, seems like the welcome witness to some approaching steamer. Wave upon wave makes tumultuous way towards us. The very song of the winds has the tone of the sea gale. But the delusion vanishes. Occasional farm houses, herds of cattle, conspicuous school buildings, barns and stacks of produce, they remind the traveler that it is a home land through which he makes his journey. When we pierce these great, productive sections, and drive miles upon miles through the gleaming fields, we forget that trees neither give us shade nor adorn the landscape. The splendor and opulence of growing grains fill the mind with such large thoughts of harvests that trees and hills and villages are forgot. They would obstruct the boundlessness of prospect and the vision of riches.

Now what kind of soil is it that gives such bounty to the Dakota farmer? The question led the National Department of Agriculture to subject samples of soil to careful analysis. The chemist gives us the result of his study and this result may be popularized in these terms: First characteristic, Dakota soil has remarkable adaptability for imbibing and retaining moisture. Second characteristic, Dakota soil contains large quantities of silica in a soluble state, and is therefore especially favorable to the raising of cereal crops. Third characteristic, the percentage of clay makes the soil the best of wheat soil, since clay supplies potash and absorbs and retains phosphoric acid, ammonia, potash, lime and other plant foods. Fourth characteristic, the soil carries an abundance of phosphoric acid. Fifth characteristic, the soil holds a large amount of nitrogen. Sixth characteristic, the soil shows a good percentage of organic matter; this not only increases the water holding power and enables Dakota to stand long droughts unharmed, but it also furnishes necessary food supply to vegetation. Dakota is surfaced by a rich, dark, alluvial loam with varying depths. Underneath is a valuable clay subsoil. The supply of soil constituents is inexhaustible. Sand and clay are mingled according to those right proportions that make the soil swift to absorb the rainfall and easy to undergo pulverization. The subsoil is not less fertile than the

top soil.   Winter frost and spring warmth operate to
the perpetual fertilization of the upper soil.   This deep
imprisoned moisture carries a burden of helpful constituents when it works its slow way to the surface.
" This soil is something wonderful, " says the editor of
the United States *Medical Investigator.* " Nature has
pursued a conservative course toward Dakota, enabling
her to hoard her wealth.   *   *   *   There is
no region that I know of with so generally rich a soil."
The fertility of the land bases the prosperity of Dakota.
That portion of the Territory east of the Missouri, and
south of the forty-sixth parallel, is under general cultivation.   The smoothness of the landscape is sometimes
broken by ranges of low hills, or the coursings of rivers,
or the bright surface of small lakes.   The mirage
plays many a trick with the traveler.   Some far away
town seems builded upon the shores of the broad lake.
And the water is high, for the very buildings seem
floating upon the surface.   But one draws nigh the
town and the waters vanish in the clouds.

When one has familiarized himself with the land,
yielded to the quiet fascination of the mighty prairies,
measured the productiveness of these smooth, rich acres,
counted the days of sunshine, drunk deep draughts of
the invigorating air, then one pardons the treeless
aspect of the country and one regards with leniency
the busy play of the winds.   At the same time any
small discontent that may suggest itself is tempered
and assuaged by the conviction that a change in these

respects already marks the lower part of the Territory and such change will gradually extend through the central portion of the land. The success which marks tree culture in Kansas, Nebraska and the Yankton district of Dakota indicates what time and work may do for other portions of the prairie country. And when the trees are grown, the winds will meet with perpetual resistance and discouragement, while rain will get such gentle wooing that Dakota will receive the unstinted irrigation of the clouds. Well-tilled lands, frequent groves, multiplied settlements, concentrated enterprises will soon convert Dakota into a mighty empire.

The climate itself will prove the ally of prosperity. Portions of this middle west are scourged by hot south winds. We were touched by them as we journeyed some hundreds of miles down the interior. They sweep over the plains with irresistible fury. They wither and scorch the harvests. They plague and discourage the farmer. But these winds have lost their riotous viciousness when they skim the Dakota fields. Their long journeys have robbed them of the power to injure. And when the evening comes they rest with the sun and give people, harvests, cattle cool, restful nights.

Dakota lies in the same latitude as several of the great rival States of the Union. Minnesota, Wisconsin, Iowa, New York, they range with Dakota. The isothermal line is an imaginary line passing through sections that have the same mean annual temperature.

This line goes westward from Harrisburg, Cleveland and Chicago, and then diverges northward through St. Paul, passing along the upper part of Dakota. Scientific observers tell us that the entire northwest is tempered by the "Chinook winds" which travel from the Indian ocean through China and Japan across the Pacific into Washington, Montana, Dakota and contiguous States.

The air is dry and freighted with ozone. Through the winter the thermometer occasionally marks 40 deg. below zero, but such cold is exceptional, and its severity is mitigated by the absence of humidity. Here is a table showing the monthly and annual mean temperature for fifteen years, of Dakota, Minnesota, New Hampshire. The cold average favors Dakota —a fact that is surprising and suggestive:

	January.	February.	March.	April.	May.	June.	July.	August.	September.	October.	November.	December.	Mean annual.
Dakota.	6.8	12.9	24.2	42.5	56 7	65.8	71.8	69 6	58.8	45.7	27.7	15.6	41.5
Minnesota	3.2	10.2	20.5	38.5	52.8	63.0	66.2	65 8	56.0	44.1	25.5	11.8	38.1
New Hampshire	6.1	8 8	9.6	20.1	34.2	44.3	46.7	47.2	42.6	30.3	17 2	11.3	26.5

We found the people frank and communicative when the winters were discussed. There seemed to be no desire on their part to deceive the traveler or pervert the truth. But Dakotaians believe that facts will right many erroneous and absurd impressions that concern their cold weather. So they insist that the facts be distributed for the enlightenment of their fellow citizens. We copy a table showing the temperature in Dakota for six months each year, (October to March,) through fourteen seasons:

1872–3	25.5°	1880–1	18.0°
1873–4	22.0	1881–2	26.8
1874–5	15.0	1882–3	21.1
1875–6	19.5	1883–4	19.6
1876–7	20.8	1884–5	20.6
1877–8	32.0	1885–6	24.0
1878–9	23.9	1886–7	17.9
1879–80	23.7		

Mean average for fifteen years.................................. 21.8°

During the winter of 1886 and 1887,taking December, January, February, there was total snowfall in Dakota of 47.8 inches; New York had a snowfall of 55.7 inches; Connecticut a snowfall of 60.5 inches ; New Hampshire a snowfall of 86. inches. These statistics fairly illustrate the winter conditions cf Dakota. In respect to mean winter temperature, amount of snowfall and bright, clear days, Dakota has precedence among various competitors. During the year 1886, Dakota had three hundred and two days that were described by observers and statisticians as fair or clear. There were only sixty-three cloudy or stormy days. This statement seems incredible. We have been prejudiced against Dakota. The length, severity, gloominess and havoc of its winters have been described with such iteration that it is hard to correct the dismal impression and yield to the force of truth. The U. S. Signal cffice furnishes the following table:

	Cloudy Days.	Clear Days.	Fair Days.	Total.
	No.	No.	No.	No.
Dakota	62.9	126.7	175.4	....
Nebraska	67.0	124.0	174.0	....
Rhode Island............	81.8	122.2	161.0	....
Kansas	83.7	135.0	146.3	... .
Minnesota...............	97.2	106.0	161.8	....
Illinois..............	102.4	115.4	147.2	....
Connecticut	103.3	113.3	148.4	....
Wisconsin...	109.1	96.8	159.1	....
Iowa.. ..	118.0	93.3	153.7	365.0
Pennsylvania............	118.8	106.2	140.0	....
Massachusetts	128.0	103.0	134.0	....
Indiana.................	128.1	94.5	142.4	... .
Maine	129.5	92.3	143.2	....
Ohio.	130.8	90.4	143.8	....
Michigan	135.3	83.1	146.6	....
New York...	153.5	76.1	135.4	....
New Hampshire..........	163.6	79.2	122.2	....

It is the universal testimony of the inhabitants of the Territory that the rigors of winter are exaggerated to such a degree that gross injustice is done the country. Investigation proves that storms are more frequent, suffering more severe, snowfall heavier and dark days more numerous in various parts of the north and west and east than they are in Dakota. This is a conclusion to which observation, statistics and personal witness force us. The north-west winds that come down from the country laden with fine particles of snow or ice— these cause the suffering and disaster that occasionally give opportunity for harsh strictures upon the storms of this northern interior. But the people are emphatic and unanimous in their statements that a real blizzard is a rare thing. Numerous residents in the Territory insist that the storm of February 12th, 1888, is the only severe storm that has visited the Territory for years. This year has been marked by unprecedented disturbances in great storm centres. The whole country has suffered. And when it occurs that New York city itself is stormed, isolated, starved, buried, paralyzed, overwhelmed by force of hostile elements, it behooves us to be quite chary of censure and criticism concerning blizzards. Not only is the New England snowfall larger, and the New England sky cloudier, and the New England winter colder, but our very blizzard is determined to surpass the trumpeted storm of the great north-west, and claims preëminence in respect to strength, cruelty, havoc. The truth is that atmospheric conditions to day are marked by singular transitions. The country is passing through phenomenal changes. New England climate is not the same that it was fifty years ago. And the north-west territory is experiencing changes. The climatic modifications of the north-west, however, are favorable to comfort, health, enjoyment. It is an open question if such statement be true concerning the climatic changes in the east.

One speedily learns that it is not climate which annoys the citizens of Dakota. Climate is a part of the Dakotaian's capital. The ozone of the air acts with healing efficacy. Dakota is a kind of illimitable, generous sanitarium. It is physician for many a broken, discouraged man. The climate woos the man into strength, energy, health. It is the monotony of tireless winds that taxes the patience and good cheer of the people. The winds rest during the night, but they are jubilantly active during the day. And yet the people make no complaint. They get accustomed to the winds. It is a part of the Dakota life. The annoyance is soon forgotten. And when the trees are multiplied as they are through the Yankton district, and the whole country has had breaking the force and persistency of the winds will be lessened. Time will modify their temper and vexatiousness. The winds will be reckoned chiefly as loyal carriers of invigorating oxygen.

The water of Dakota deserves special notice. Water is an important factor in the development of any country. Dakota has many lakes and rivers. The water surface of the Territory is reckoned at 1,400 square miles. The rainfall of the country increases annually. The average rainfall for the five months of April, May, June, July and August through a period of seven years has been 14.89 inches. But it is artesian wells that make Dakota's water privileges especially notable. These wells are operated all through South Dakota. Yankton has twelve or fourteen of them. They yield an immense flow. The pressure is so great that the water is carried through the streets and into the houses. The pressure is so great that heavy machinery is successfully operated. A six-inch well in Yankton, recently completed, furnishes power to the machinery of a pressed brick manufactory. The well yields 1,800 gallons per minute—giving a pressure equal to thirty-three horse power. The well at Huron gives a pressure equivalent to a hundred horse power. The cost of sinking these wells is not so great that their use is impracticable. Their rapid multiplication evidences their worth, utility, profit. Twenty-nine counties in the Territory have already used artesian wells. The system is destined to take important part in the history of the country. At the session of the Territorial Legislature in 1887 a law was enacted which provides for the construction and support of artesian wells in townships and cities by an assessment upon the property holders and residents. The character of the water used for drinking and cooking purposes varies in different parts of the country. Some residents prefer cistern water. Various mineral substances give tone to the great share of the well water. Dr. Duncan, of Chicago, notes especially the restorative properties of the Dakota waters. For many weaknesses and diseases he writes that they rival the famous springs of the east. The water problem has been satisfactorily solved for Dakota. We remember that not only has the soil marvellous powers of moisture retention, but the rains themselves are graciously enlarging their precious ministry.

And this is the Dakota land—level, stoneless, afflu·ent, profitable—making good response to the courtship of the farmer, witnessing to the benefits of large cultivation and industrious conquest—a land that shall prove the matchless farm land of the fair great west.

DAKOTA RESOURCES.

The products of the soil are numerous. Wheat makes first claim upon us. In respect to quantity of wheat, Dakota leads the States. One-thirtieth part of the Territory was sown to grain in 1887. An acreage of 3,818,752 yielded an average of 16⅓ bushels of wheat to the acre. The crop amounted to 62,553,499 bushels. This was a gain of some 70 or 100 per cent. over the yield of the preceding year.

The soil itself is especially adapted to the raising of wheat. It abounds in those constituents that are compacted into the bread grain. Dakota climate favors the prosperity of this valuable cereal. The heat of summer and the cold of winter—the moisture of earth and the invigoration of air—contribute their help and impulse. The very seasons seem arranged with a view to the superlative merit and prodigal harvest of the grain.

But it is not only quantity of wheat that is note-worthy; quality of wheat is an important factor. The Dakota grain reveals a dryness and richness of albuminoids that give it the first rank in the market. The Bureau of Chemistry of the United States Department of Agriculture has analyzed the various wheat products of the country. " Dakota wheat," says the report " makes a flavor richer than any other." Experiment proves that a bushel of Dakota wheat will make more bread than a bushel of wheat from any other section of the country and that this bread contains a larger percentage of the materials which nourish the human body, than the bread made from any other wheat. The Dakota wheat is all of the spring varieties. The farmer therefore evades certain perils to the crop that are incident to the raising of winter wheat.

This Dakota wheat also brings a larger price than any of its competitors. It is worth from five to ten cents more per bushel than any other wheat. It rules the market. The drift of conversation in Minneapolis and Duluth is in the direction of Dakota wheat. It seems to bear the closest relation to all trade and enterprise. And this same grain that commands the highest market price is raised at such low price of production as to discredit all wheat culture in the eastern States. The average land investment of the Dakota farmer is the small sum of $5.90 per acre. The New York man reckons his land at $46 an acre ; the Ohio man at $44 an acre. Here is striking disparity. Then the work of cultivating the eastern farm is a larger and more expensive thing. Taxes and interest put the Dakota man at another advantage. The comparative results are easily stated. The Dakota farmer distances his New York competitor and drives him out of the market. It is the inevitable issue. The east cannot compete with the west when it comes to the question of profitable farming.

But this same Dakota wheat is now transported to the centres of trade at small cost. This is another important factor. Duluth will speedily become the great wheat market of the world. Some eight or ten railroads already centre in the "Zenith City." Some ten other roads are under process of construction. Some ten other roads are projected and will doubtless emerge into visibility within five years. And this great network of railroads reaches through Dakota and brings the Territory into close communication with the water-ways of the east. Duluth is from 200 to 350 miles nearer Dakota than Chicago. Wheat is shipped from Duluth at a great saving. The whole cost of wheat transportation from Dakota to Buffalo will soon be reduced to 15 cents per bushel, says a prominent dealer. Here we note a tremendous saving to the Dakota farmer and a mighty impulse to the wheat culture of the Territory. Railroad transportation of wheat to the east costs nearly three times as much as water transportation.

The wheat crop of Dakota brings a magnificent and substantial income to the farmers. And yet wheat culture is simply making its small beginnings in the Territory. When the land is all put under cultivation—all put under thorough, scientific cultivation, the yield will become enormous. Dakota will feed the nation with bread and grow opulent while gladly meeting the necessities of man.

But such emphasis is put upon wheat that one well nigh forgets how the Dakota lands yield diversified crops. Sioux City, Iowa, built her Corn Palace in the autumn of 1887. It was an ingenious, beautiful, suggestive structure. As an artistic triumph in corn it proved memorable. And it served the purpose of directing attention to this important centre of agricultural traffic. But Sioux City borders upon Dakota and its immense supplies of farm produce are partly gleaned from the Dakota fields. Corn itself is becoming a characteristic crop of the Territory. The Sioux City Corn Palace was in part a matter of homage to the Dakota prairies. Three years have witnessed a marked change in respect to the work methods of the Territorial farmers. When Dakota was first advertised by its remarkable wheat harvests, men gave no thought to other crops. It was all wheat. The opinion prevailed that it was a one crop country. The risks incident to a one crop country were boldly faced and the development of the Territory was rapid. But the American farmer carries his wits with him. He is born to make shrewd experiment, and when corn was planted and the corn acres were multiplied, it was discovered that if corn was not king, corn stood near the throne. The harvest of 1887 yielded some 25,000,000 of bushels. This is a larger corn crop than that of New York or Min-

nesota, or South Carolina, or twenty-two other of the
States and Territories.

The quality of the corn is excellent. Analysis
shows that it is especially rich in albuminoids and
nitrogen. The soil and the climate are both agreeable
to the cereal. The average yield is forty bushels to
the acre.

Flax is another crop that promises well in Dakota.
The yield for 1886 was 3,844,788 bushels. The seed
is the only part that is utilized to-day, but the time
will speedily come when shops and factories will work
the fibre into marketable form. Paper, cordage, lin-
seed oil, paints, cloth, twine are consumed in large
quantities by the people of Dakota. These articles all
come from the east. When Dakota learns to manufacture them herself the flax crop will become a very
profitable investment.

Rye, oats, barley and buckwheat are also the products of the Territory, although their cultivation is a matter of recent trial. The rye crop of 1887 was 316,586
bushels; the barley crop 6,400,568 bushels; the
buckwheat crop 97,230 bushels, and the oat crop 43,-
267,478 bushels. Oats yield a harvest varying from
sixty to ninety bushels per acre. Rye averages from
thirty-five to fifty bushels per acre. Dakota comes near
to taking the lead in respect to oats. One farmer related
to the writer, how in 1882 he sowed a ten acre patch with
oats, and reaped 730 bushels for his harvest. As the

oats sold for 33 cents per bushel he got a return of
$24.09 per acre for his work.

The vegetables of Dakota deserve notice. The
size, quality and abundance of the garden products
astonish the stranger. Potatoes grow to an enormous size. They yield from 150 to 300 bushels per
acre. People show potatoes that weigh six pounds.
This year the farmers of Dakota have supplied many of
their neighbors with this season's vegetables. Indiana
itself has used Dakota potatoes. The crop is always
sure, say the farmers, the quality of the potatoe
being the finest. Its superiority will get it good
market in the east, so that the better price will
pay the cost of transportation. Onions yield from 400
to 800 bushels an acre. Turnips, peas, beans, carrots,
parsnips, lettuce, radishes, melons, cauliflower and
beets are raised with good results. At the Territorial
Fair, in Mitchell, in 1887, cabbages were exhibited which
weighed between thirty and forty pounds. Pumpkins
were exhibited which tipped the scales at 200 pounds.
It would appear that the vegetables do not propose to
be outdone by the vastness of the Territory. They will
show the ambitious western spirit and excel the east
after a fashion that matches the immensity of the Territorial field.

The native grasses of Dakota are nutritious and
abundant. Hay time does not signify to these people
the same work that it does to the eastern farmer.
The prairie supply of hay suffices for everybody.

c

The hay crop of 1887 reached 2,500,000 tons. Large quantities were exported. The task of cutting and stacking the hay is done whenever the farmer finds the time to turn from the harvest duties. Often the standing grass furnishes nourishment to cattle all through the winter. "Cattle come out of the Bad Lands in the Spring," writes E. V. Smalley, "as fat as though they had been stall-fed all winter." Timothy, millett, alfalfa flourish in the Territory. In fact, native grasses and imported grasses yield bountiful returns, and make Dakota a desirable land for dairy purposes.

Sugar beets give admirable results. Scientific men propose to encourage that profitable industry. If sugar can be made from this product of Dakota soil, the sugar interests of the country may receive very important modification. Experiment will determine the matter.

Fruit culture is in its infancy, but enough has been done to show the fine possibilities of soil and climate in the raising of numerous fruits.

Dakota is destined to become a famous stock country. The lay of the land, the invigoration of the climate, the growth of succulent grasses, the general adaptability of the country to herds and dairies, indicate Dakota as a promiseful stock region. The cattle business is yet in the incipient state. People have been so controlled by the wheat interest that they have not adjusted themselves to the fact that stock will give good profits among them. The live stock that was reckoned for the year 1887 is valued at $43,195,229.

This is no mean showing for an industry that has just made its beginning. The past seven years has increased the live stock of the Territory by an investment of more than $36,000,000. Dakota already surpasses thirty States and Territories in the extent and and largeness of her cattle industry. The great pork packing establishments of Omaha and Sioux City and Minneapolis draw immense supplies from Dakota. Pork packing is a business that will soon employ thousands of men in the Territory itself.

"I will challenge any man," a prosperous farmer of Central Dakota writes us, "to show better horses, cattle, sheep, in the States than we have raised here in Spink county." And our observation sustains this farmer's statement. There are millions of acres of native forage interspersed through the Territory. Hogs thrive upon it through the summer and autumn. The large corn harvests are easily converted into swine's flesh when the need of such food comes. Nearly 500,-000 hogs were fattened in the Territory in 1886.

Cattle are observed scattered all along the prairies. The dry and even weather of the summer favors the health and vigor of the animals. The luxuriant grasses afford fat nourishment. When it is time to sell the herd the beef packing establishments gather them into their sheds. The farmer's task is done and his cattle are converted into dollars. But not all cattle are disposed of according to this summary fashion. Milk, butter and cheese are now staple commodities of

the Territory. Here and there you observe creameries
and cheese factories. Every farmer has his company of
animals (small or large as the case may be). It witnesses to the general character and diverse products of
the farm work. The perils of failure are lessened to
such degree that one now feels good assurance of live-
lihood and profit whatever turn may be given to affairs
by peculiarities of season.

One is also pleased to see the frequent flocks of
sheep that appear in various parts of the Territory.
This is new business. There were few sheep in Dakota
seven years ago. The brief experiment in raising sheep
has been eminently successful. As the facts are
scattered among the farmers there will result a notable
increase in the number and size of the herds and the
product of the wool. "I do not believe there is a
better country in the world for sheep," remarked an
enterprising farmer who had made good success with
his flocks.

As we travel through the Territory and observe the
swift development of these various agricultural industries, we are profoundly impressed by the great
possibilities of the field. There are only 75,000 acres of
the "Bad Lands" in all the Territory. These "Bad
Lands" afford nutritious pasturage to great droves of
cattle. Dakota, we learn, has less waste land in
proportion to its size than any other State or Territory in
the Union. As we follow the trend of life, measure
the force of work, reckon the opportunities for ex-

pansion, ponder the opulence of nature, we are in-
spired with an indomitable faith in the future greatness
of this majestic Territory.

But the resources of Dakota are not confined to
agriculture. Dakota is emphatically and preëminently
an agricultural land, yet there must inevitably come a
development of other resources that shall prove helpful.
Brick making, paper making, broom making, wagon
making, flour mills, feed mills, iron mills, planing
mills, woolen mills, saw mills, shingle mills, glass
factories, paint factories, sash and door factories,
foundries, marble works, packing houses, we observe
all these industries, and although they are yet infant
enterprises, they represent a capital of $11,000,000.
Dakota will do a large part of her own shop work, give
her time to develop the business. The home supply of
raw material is so large and the home consumption
reaches such enormous proportions that economy and
thrift will force the Dakotaian into manufactures.

There are the mines of the Territory. They signify
work, population, trade, wealth. The country west of
the Missouri as well as a good part of North Dakota
contains a rich deposit of coal. The soft variety is
especially abundant. While inferior to anthracite, it
nevertheless will supply the people with cheap, good
fuel. In the neighborhood of the Black Hills there are
immense deposits of coal. It is said that the Great
Sioux reservation is especially rich in this mineral.
The time will soon come when Dakota will heat herself

by her own treasured fires. The gold and silver products of the Black Hills are important contributions to
the resources of the Territory. The Homestake mine
has paid dividends to the amount of $3,843,750; the
Father de Smet has paid dividends to the amount of
$1,125,000 ; numerous other mines have yielded
fair profits. Railroads will give a tremendous impulse to the careful and profitable working of the
various ores that are prodigally scattered through the
Black Hills. Tin was discovered in 1883. Time will
reveal the importance of this discovery. Other valuable ores are found. One is safe in prophesying a
prosperous future for this part of Dakota. A country
that will yield nearly $34,000,000 worth of gold and
silver in a period of ten years, and that combines with
her mining interests a fair share of agricultural and
trade interests, gives unequivocal promise of greatness.

We get a good interpretation of Dakota's substantial resources when we note the financial condition of
the Territory. The wealth of Dakota exceeds $350,-
000,000. (Computed by Territorial officials.) The past
seven years has noted an annual increase of $40,000,-
000 in the real values of the Territory. Farm improvements, immigration, the building of houses, construction of railroads, reveal the secret of such property expansion. Railroads pierce the land at the rate of a
thousand miles per year. This year the immigration
is computed at one hundred thousand people. The
various trade centres of the different counties show an

unprecedented activity and growth. The land itself promises a wealth of harvests that has stimulated the farmer into the largest hopefulness. In 1875 Dakota school property was valued at $25,000. Twelve years expand these figures into $3,000,000. In May, 1887, Dakota issued bonds to the amount of $400,000, bearing four and a half per cent. interest. These bonds were sold at a premium of more than half of one per cent. Dakota now places her securities at a rate of interest lower than that ever obtained by any other Territory. The financial soundness of Dakota commends her bonds, her character, her products, her people.

DAKOTA PEOPLE.

It is a delicate matter when one has sojourned among the people of a new land, to speak candidly and judiciously concerning individuals and classes. But the people have made Dakota the prosperous land which we have seen. And the people deserve a share of study and remark in connection with such noble task. One is speedily impressed with the fact that the people are young. It is a land where all affairs seem conducted by men who are rugged with the strength of first manhood. The west itself is exuberant and masterful through this sovereignty of stalwart and ambitious youth. The farms are pioneered by young men. The churches are builded by young men. The banks are managed by young men. The stores, the shops, the schools, the railroads, are run by young men. Law, politics, medicine, religion, they all centre in young men. And it is neither to the discredit of the young men nor to the discredit of work, trade, profession, that we say it. The nine hundred young men who faced Frederick Barbarossa on the plains beyond Milan, and won the day for Milanese independence, did a work that symbols the possible achievement of youth when their strength and enthusiasm centre upon life's tasks. Young men pursue the course of nature when

they join themselves to these western conquerors and
go forth to subdue the land. There is something
peculiarly stimulating in this association with invin-
cible manhood. Imagination is a loyal servant through
the days of youth. And one needs imagination to push
one's way through some of the labors that appeal to the
western settler. The old house was probably guarded
by oaks and elms and maples. Their shade soothed
the body when the summer days grew warm. But
Dakota trees are largely objects of the imagination.
Give them time and they will grace the new made home
and sing their gentle monotones to the inmates. To-
day, however, one must imagine their grace and music.
And so with various creature comforts that administer
to the contentment of age. Young men see these things
in their mind's eye. A little tarrying upon time and
the mighty prairies shall give the people ample shade,
tempered breezes, refreshing showers, all the amenities
of the former life. There is precious refreshment to
the Dakota citizen in this subtle ministry of the imagination.

The traveler meets few men who have passed the
age of fifty. The prime of life gives its unforgetable
stamp to the development of the land. And it does
not appear that these people lack wise counsel and
good balance. They show sense, practicality, purpose-
fulness, toned by the vastness of the landscape and the
invigoration of the air.

We note the courage of the Dakotaians. It may be

that the ruggedness of the winters does something for
them in the making of courage. The rough usage of
a blizzard is undoubtedly conducive to a spirit of
brave and stubborn resistance. A repetition of March
12th, 1888, in New York, may serve the same general
end through the east. When one has withstood such
an assault of the elements it sometimes quickens into
vigor certain qualities of mind that are essential to the
successful life. These Dakota people manifest a courage that gives character to plans, labors, experiences.
"Are you not timid, living away from neighbors here
in the prairie," we say to the farmer's wife. And she
replies, "we are only a mile or two miles from such a
house. The school is near. Neighbors grow more
common. We have nothing to fear. Harm never
touches us. We are not annoyed by tramps. We
scarce ever see an Indian. They stay upon their re-
servations." Such is common testimony. But there
are many transactions that require courage. Work,
privation, economy, discomfort, it takes courage to
face these things. So it occurs that the faint heart
fails and returns to the narrowness and the discontent
of the east.

Dakota people are alert to the demands of the day.
Their energy. is attributable in some degree to the
stimulation of the climate. They agree with Napo-
leon that the dictionary does not contain the word
" can't." The Dakotaian is always ready to say with
Frederick of Prussia, " I dare to do the impossible."

And when you think of it, it appears that their achievements have been along that line. There are nearly five thousand miles of railroads in the Territory to-day. And the roads are pushing through the farm districts in all directions. The settlers are not obliged to caravan their way to their new homes. The cars distribute them along the very land that they propose to till. The old time pioneer life is foreign to the present settlement of Dakota. It was the general opinion when the Territory was first advertised that wheat was the only crop congenial to the soil. This was a thing that demanded investigation. It was not long ere experiment proved the generous character of the soil and its adaptability to the interests of varied farming. The meagre water supply annoyed the settlers. They studied the nature of their farm grounds and learned that the moisture of summer and winter was retained with unexampled persistency, so that the bugbear drought was driven into exile. Still, the moisture of the deep soil did not signify precious streams of crystal water. They therefore pierced the earth with artesian wells until great strong volumes of the desired fluid pushed their way through the earth's surface and carried blessings to the land. But it does not matter what the demand ; these people show the enterprise to meet it. There is nothing in the way of practicable achievement which they will not master, give them time to do it. And they pursue their course with such an air of quiet, equable self-confidence that the traveler

is shamed into faith. As you meet these people you
feel the throb of a swift, earnest, aggressive, triumphant life, and how cordial these lively people are!

We made our first entrance into Dakota through
Watertown. It was a gray and misty morning. The
fields were wet with recent rains. The landscape
presented a sobriety and melancholy that did not
conduce to good cheer or light-heartedness. As the
train drew near the depot we saw throngs of men. The
city was a-throb with tumultuous life, and when the
train stopped we were greeted with the resonant,
exultant strains of a brass band. The grayness of the
morning and the melancholy of the landscape were
forgotten. We had read that when men visited this
new west the people were bound to make favorable
impression upon them. We had even read that
when men sought this new west with an eye to business
and development they were greeted by brass bands.
But we had always thought such stories apocryphal,
and here was the plain fact which our skeptical mind
had disputed. The band played with all the expression
and enthusiasm that it was possible for them to put into
their interpretation of " Hail to the Chief." We were
touched by the spontaneity and the cordiality of such
unexpected greeting. And then just as the contagion
had communicated itself to us and we were preparing
to pass a vote of thanks, we discovered that it was a
political convention that had been thrust upon us and
we withdrew into the obscurity of our small company

and again thought upon the grayness of the morning and the melancholy of the landscape. Nevertheless the people do greet one with a happy heartiness that is all their own.

Can it be that the genial play of Dakota sunshine incarnates itself in the person of its people? Driving through the endless fields of wheat, corn and oats we hailed the farmer and discussed his work. That does not satisfy the man; we must go into the house; we must share his modest hospitality; we must measure the profit and the satisfaction of a 1,000 acre Dakota farm. It was the same spirit of good cheer, large fellowship, happy welcome, whether we journeyed in the cars or tarried at the hotels or mingled with the people in their houses. The newness, the largeness, the importance of their tasks give them a certain fine spirit of comradeship. They want to share their responsibilities with their fellows. They want to divide opportunities among their associates. Rivalry itself among them seems generous and true hearted. One necessarily finds a great deal of personal competition among the people who make these new communities. But the bitterness and harassment of feud and quarrel have not yet dimmed the youth of the fair land. The large productive charity that features the literature of the New Testament makes forceful appeal to the free life of the West. Its adaptability to the anomalous conditions of society is a very suggestive fact. Dakota is favored with a wealth of fair and cloudless days. Weather *will* thrust itself into the moods, features, energies and characters of men.

It were a matter of course to remark the intelligence of these people. They publish 352 newspapers. This number exceeds the number published in twenty-four different States of the Union. Intelligence were palpable in the very fact that these people have sought this fertile land and chosen it as the home-place. New York farms represent an average investment of $46 per acre. Dakota farms represent an average investment of $6 per acre. The Dakota acre will surpass the New York acre in productiveness. And the New York markets, by the help of water-ways, serve the Dakota farmer when he sells his produce. These settlers of South Dakota, are predominantly American. They came from all the eastern States. They represent the best families of the land. It is not frontier pandemonium that one finds in Dakota. The people bring books, pictures, pianos with them,—all the accessories of refinement and education. Their small homes are filled with the evidences of mental culture. The magazines, the reviews, the newspapers, are conveniently at hand. Dakota life seems to sharpen the wits of these people. There is just enough adventure connected with a migration westward to spice the life, and give it a healthful invigoration. The mind becomes active, observant, efficient. And the innumerable questions that concern life when the community passes through its formative season, call into activity the faculties that might otherwise lie quiescent. One could not but notice the extent of general information and the accuracy of statement revealed through gen-eral conversation. People have the feeling that they must do their own thinking in Dakota. It may be that some of the pioneers chose the Territory for a home with that very purpose. The conservatism and the conventionality of the East depressed them and trammeled them. Here they have the freedom of the prairies. And they can put this thought into the plastic conditions of this fresh life. It not only gives men satisfaction, but it fosters mind-power, this taking share in the making of the State. Circumstances were important factors in determining the sturdy, indepen-dent, noble type of our New England ancestry. And circumstances contribute their strength to the worth and character of the Dakota people.

The Territory is marked by a significant patriotism. Many thousands of our soldiers have chosen Dakota for their home-making. We meet them on every side. And sometimes it is a pathetic sight. It is farming under difficulties when the man has only one arm to help him, or when infirmity makes the days uncertain and distressful. You see these people scattered through Dakota. They fought the country's battles, and they accept the country's dole of land and bread. There is no charity about this thing. It is meagre, petty pay-ment for a service that saved the integrity of the

Union. And these same soldiers, who braved death for their country, who carry wound scars that stamp them with the honorable insignia of patriotism, are disfranchised. They take no part in the peaceful administration of this Government. They pay their taxes, submit to distant domination, and endure the shame and contumely of voiceless, helpless insignificance. It speaks well for the loyalty of the Dakota people that they pursue a dignified, straightforward course. Hope is strong in the hearts of these citizens. They carry with them positive assurance that the future shall bring them unstinted prosperity. These people have observed the trend of events. They have measured the promises of the years. Disappointment may touch them; circumstances may vex them, but their unfaltering faith in the country, and their indomitable reliance upon themselves, make them triumphantly hopeful. Foreigners have not settled largely in South Dakota. The native American has impressed the country with his unique character. And as you move among these people, you confess to an atmosphere of prosperity that seems to brood above the very land and give its healthful impulse to the tiller of the soil as well as the citizen of the town. It is delightful to tarry with people who make perpetual distribution of good cheer, large faith, cordial spirit, happy zeal. It is worth the journey to this Dakota land—a few days' association with such largeness of plan, enthusiasm of progress, magnitude of achievement. It was the saying of the old Greek poet,

Epaminondas, that "the gods sell for labor all good things." These modern Dakotaians give fine emphasis to the classic maxim.

One does not look for many charitable, religious and educational institutions in a country that has just been subdued. These witnesses to advanced civilization are things of slow growth. Nevertheless, we found them in Dakota. The zeal of these people is especially noticeable when you discuss reform, education, religion. Various institutions for the amelioration of suffering and the reformation of the depraved have been founded and supported by the territory. Asylums, penitentiaries, prisons, are conducted on the plans that approve themselves to the intelligence of the people, and their work bears very favorable comparison with neighbor States. It is a suggestive fact, however, that the percentage of criminals confined in the penitentiaries is the smallest of any State in the Union, being only 1 to 2,253 inhabitants.

Church work shows an energy, an aggressiveness, an enthusiasm that touch the observer to the quick. A great task is laid upon the various missionary societies. The new towns demand church privileges. They have not had time to do much in the way of public improvement; private affairs have occupied their first days. But the church necessity presses itself into the heart. The people ask the help of their Eastern friends. The Missionary Society sends its men. The field is canvassed, a loan is made to the young church, a

D

modest edifice is erected and the town is strengthened
by this compact and visible expression of the religious
sentiment. The villages and the cities all have their
churches. They are among the first signs of a genuine
home life. These modest beginnings contain the potency
of great, vigorous organizations. Speedily growing into
self-support, they operate with tremendous power in the
shaping of the people into worthy character. And
still the work does not keep pace with the demands of
the day. It is the season of supreme opportunity.
The church as a precious factor in the moulding of these
new, sensitive conditions is welcomed and cherished.
But the missionary societies seem blind to the magnificent fields that stretch before them, or is it the
people of the east who fail to measure the importance
of the formative period, and so give small contributions
to these societies that plant and foster young churches?
These western workmen who direct church affairs show
a zeal, earnestness, self-denial, enterprise that fill the
traveler with admiration and inspire him with hope ;
nevertheless, their tasks expand with such speed and
attain such vast proportions, that discouragement
sometimes perils their devotion and threatens to stare
them out of countenance. Men drive their thirty and
forty miles on the Sabbath, preaching morning, afternoon
and evening, ministering to three and sometimes four
congregations, conducting Sunday schools, organizing
neighborhood meetings, planning the prosperity of
churches. And these herculean labors are performed

with a good cheer and an enthusiasm that give happy witness to the worth and meaning of such labors. But it is something that must be dinned into the ears and pushed into the hearts of our eastern people, that now is the accepted time. This new west may be wrought into a strength, merit, beauty of Christian civilization that shall make it the very paradise of the Republic. Will the church do it? Make generous, triumphant response, wise and loyal citizens of this great country!

Dakota's educational institutions are numerous and progressive. The public school system advantages the the Territory after a noble fashion. We observed three handsome district school houses a short distance from Redfield that cost some $4,000 (the three buildings). Four thousand public schools are scattered through the prairies.

Dakota surpasses eight States and all the Territories in school population. She employs a greater number of school teachers than sixteen of the States. She has more school days than eleven States. The value of her school property exceeds that of thirty-three States and Territories. She enrolls a larger percentage of the children in her schools than any other State or Territory, with the exception of Connecticut, Florida, Massachusetts, Nevada, New Hampshire and Rhode Island. Each township has 1,280 acres set apart by the United States Government for the support of public schools. These lands are available when the Territory attains statehood. As the lands are valued approximately at $5,000,000 according to the Commissioner of Immigration, the sale of these lands would give the largest school fund belonging to any State. At the present time the nearly $2,000,-000 devoted to school work is annually raised by taxation and the people bear the burden without complaint. These public schools keep abreast of the times. The methods of instruction and the class of text books denote that teachers are well trained and thoroughly posted. Special instruction is here given concerning the nature and effects of alcoholic drinks and narcotics, although nearly sixty counties have banished the saloon and illustrate local prohibition.

Higher institutions of learning are established in different parts of the Territory. The various sections will soon have their own academies and colleges, so that a thorough education is possible to any industrious, ambitious youth. There are seven Territorial institutions and fourteen other colleges and academies. Handsome buildings have been erected by many of these schools. We could not visit them, but we met a number of the men who have the leadership in educational affairs, and the reports which they gave us showed the usefulness and the influence of the institutions. Yankton College has done an excellent work. The President, Doctor Ward, is a man of rare ability, one who does not restrict labor to academic halls, but shares loyally in all public enterprises. President Ward has invested a large amount of personal labor in the numerous affairs that concern the prosperity and character of South Dakota. The University at Vermillion enters heartily into the work of the day. The institution gives fine promise of State service under the leadership of its popular, energetic President. Redfield College is a school that has recently been founded in Redfield, Spink county. The location is good and the opportunities of service are numerous. Its President shows great zeal in his task of organization. The building recently erected for the use of the institution is one of the handsomest edifices that we saw in Dakota. Like other new schools established in the Territory it illustrates the thrift, enterprise, self-sacrifice, intelligence of its loyal founders and benefactors. Men make no happier or profitabler investment of their money than in the solid construction and thorough organization of such institutions. Redfield College, Grotan College, Sioux Falls University, Pierre University, Dakota University, Yankton College—they all deserve the large bounty and the cordial support of eastern and western friends. These institutions are vital to the mental vigor and moral health of the Territory. College graduates are numerous in Dakota. They are alive to the significance of higher education. They propose that this broad commonwealth shall source its future greatness in the large intelligence and the regal merit of its people.

DAKOTA CITIES.

An eastern man uses the word city with diffidence when he refers to the larger towns of the Territory. People who are accustomed to villages of 10,000 inhabitants, like Stamford, Ct., or 15,000 inhabitants like Saratoga Springs, do not easily adjust their speech to the western conditions. But the matter rights itself after one gets familiar with the situation. A man must visit Duluth, Minneapolis, Kansas City, Omaha, Sioux City, and other places that have made their history during the last five or fifteen years. He must glean statistics, study territory, measure trade possibilities, remark the ultimate centre of immigration. When this has been done with faithfulness, he has data for judgment in respect to cities. The slow, staid, ancient, monotonous movements of the New England farm districts are not characteristic of western life. Dakota abounds in "rustlers." And we are prepared to say "city" when we describe these busy, workful, energetic, thriving, wonderful towns.

The thing that first impresses us when we get good understanding of the thing is the reasonableness of the claim to cityhood. Dakota is an immense Territory. It is rapidly passing under the sway of the farmer. Well nigh seven hundred thousand people make Dakota their home. Such tremendous influx of settlers necessitates the building of cities. There are fifteen or eighteen towns that lay just claim to that name in the Territory. And that is a small number for a great State containing 150,000 square miles of land. Now, these cities are all small. They are young. They have not had time to gain a large population. They have never been marked by sporadic, high-pressure, abnormal development. Mining towns spring into existence in a day, and then die almost as quickly. Mining districts do not conduce to health and vigor of city growth. The fever and uncertainty connected with the business impart their own peculiar features to the towns. But these Dakota cities are the inevitable results of agricultural prosperity. In the first place, we observe that the rapid development of the country necessitated trade centres. The farmer must have a convenient post where he can obtain supplies, transact the necessary business of food, clothes, implements, stock. As the districts became settled, the trade centres grew in importance. Five years make these trade centres veritable cities, although their population may not have attained great numbers The character of the place is civic. Its relations to the country are civic. The atmosphere is civic. Banks, stores, hotels, factories, offices, shops, newspapers, activities and enterprises, all tend to give the trade centre a city worth and prominence. The territory which these places drain is enormous. Counties that exceed some of the eastern States

in size contribute all their business to a city such as we
have described.   The amount of business transacted as-
tonishes the traveler.   Two dry goods stores situated in
one of the newest of these places (a town that does not
yet call itself a city,) did a business last year that a
mounted to $40,000 each.   These figures indicate the
trade possibilities of the Dakota trade centres.   It is a
matter of necessity that each section of the country
build such a town to centralize its interests.

   The railroad corporations are swift to interpret this
need.   When they pierce the land they plan these occasional centres.   With an eye to their own prosperity
they establish a town, making large grants of land to it,
encouraging the settlement of the place, giving generously to the erection of public buildings and doing
many things to multiply the attractions of the centre.
The railroad corporations have transformed the great
west into an industrious, energetic, profitable country.
These corporations enhance the value of their own
property and enlarge their business at the same time
that they prove allies of the tradesmen and farmers in
the great task of making a rich and prosperous commonwealth.   These cities become railroad centres.
Take such a place as Aberdeen.   The Milwaukee, St.
Paul, Chicago road, the Northwestern road, the Mani-
toba road, the Aberdeen & Bismarck road meet each
other here.   This illustrates the condition.   When
one road has entered a thriving central town other
roads are compelled to push for the same place.   These

corporations show remarkable shrewdness and fore-sight in such matters. And the men who direct their affairs have impregnable confidence in the future im-portance of these elected cities. In frequent conversa-tions with railroad officials, we were profoundly im-pressed by their mighty faith in Dakota's greatness. Pivotal points—that is what the railroads make these cities. The roads diverge from them in all directions. They are rapidly cutting the landscape into small sec-tions. They transport the commodities of life to the very door of the farmers, and then take in exchange his wheat, oats, potatoes, corn, cattle and butter.

These central cities are also county seats. The public offices and buildings must be located where they are convenient to the people. Trade centres and railroad centres have decided the question of con-venience. The county business therefore adds its strength to the prosperity of the favored cities. Pro-fessional men are naturally attracted to these places. They observe opportunities such as are rare and promiseful. Education gets an impulse that signifies thorough work and broad culture. The various advantages that pertain to the life of aggressive cities are common to these nascent Dakota towns. We recognize their right to sisterhood among the cities of the land. "How large are your city limits?" we said to a citizen who spoke enthusiastically concerning the growth of his town. "Three miles square," was the reply. "Is not that pretty large territory for you?"

"No," he said. "We have well nigh spread over all that space, and in a short time we shall be obliged to stretch the city limits." The truth of it is, these cities grow with such vigorous rapidity that a stranger is incompetent to discuss the merits of their case.

Dakota is an agricultural Territory. It is farm work that explains her marvellous prosperity. Nevertheless, there are splendid opportunities for the development of manufacturing interests. Such a vast country must do a good share of its own shop work if it proposes to manage its affairs with economy. Milling is a business that will grow into good proportions in these cities. There are already one hundred and fourteen flouring mills in the Territory. Farm work is done by machinery. The amount of farm machinery sent annually into Dakota is enormous. It represents a great amount of money that is sent out of Dakota. A fair share of such implements will be made in the Territory itself ere many years pass. Railroad shops give employment to many men in the cities. The brick yards, the broom factories, the feed mills, the tow mills, the carriage shops, the wood shops and other manufacturing establishments are making good beginnings. But mechanical and factory industries are not thoroughly established. The cities are alive to the demands of the hour. They will now give special encouragement to these enterprises, but the immediate necessities of the farmers and the task of building up trade have so engrossed the people that manufacturing interests have not received the support and gained the impetus that shall be given to them in the future. As we pass from town to town we remark the next step in the regal prosperity of Dakota. The cities must foster manufactures. Such a course will fill them with industrious, intelligent artisans, give strength and stability to the city institutions, supply the home consumption of many valuable products, enlarge and stimulate the circulation of money and share very generously in the prosperity of the commonwealth. Aberdeen is well located for purposes of manufacture. We do not mean that it has water power. These Dakota cities— the most of them—must depend upon steam or electricity or artesian wells for motive in machine work. But Aberdeen commands a wide section of country, and the railroads make it a centre. Trade flows easily to it, the influx of people is large and continuous. The city shows a liveliness, an enterprise, a persistency, a decision that commend it to men of like instincts and purposes. The activity among the builders is remarkable. Private houses, business blocks, railroad shops, public edifices, they are all in process of erection and still the demand outstrips the supply. Watertown, near the eastern boarder of the Territory, has a location that is especially attractive. The monotony of a level country is avoided by the gentle rise of low hills on the one side and an undulating, elevated landscape on the other. There is just enough diversity of surface to rest and please the eye. The city gathers into its

limits the central plain and the neighboring elevations.
The broad, straight streets press their way into the
prairies or run their course down to the low shores of
the modest Big Sioux river.   Here one notes the same
air of brisk trade and enthusiastic enterprise.   Handsome residences rise in various parts of the city.   The
lawns will be neat and trim and shaded when time
gives full encouragement to man's workmanship.   But
people feel that they can afford to wait, and one for-
gives the crudeness and the freshness of the work
when we measure the promise of the future.   Shaded
streets and beautiful lawns—they are the precious
fruition of years.   Watertown is less than ten years
old.   Yet it has reached proportions that give perfect
assurance of its permanent character.   The finest bank
building in the Territory adorns one of the streets of
the city.   And we were surprised to see many handsome stores, offices, blocks, buildings, giving the place
an appearance of worth, stability, progress that might
well be the envy of eastern cities.   It will not be long
ere the wholesale trade will gain a foothold in this
energetic town.   A vast country is tributary to Watertown.   Its growth will necessarily be rapid during the
next decade.

One of the attractions here is Lake Kampeska.   A
beautiful piece of landscape stretches between the city
and the lake.   As one stands upon the elevation northward one observes the gleaming waters in the distance.
We drive through three miles of undulating verdure,

and then we rest on the pleasant shores of Kampeska. Jutting cliffs, ample fields, fringes of trees, occasional cottages, such is the narrow bordering of the lake, but great broad lands of living green give the ampler framing to the beautiful retreat. Kampeska is destined to give delightful prominence to Watertown. The motor line in process of construction, which will connect the city and the lake, promises to make a summer resort of large proportions and wide fame. Add trade activities, railroad facilities, manufacturing interests, and Kampeska enjoyments, and the sum will be a large, flourishing, important, attractive city named Watertown.

Some sixty miles west the traveler finds Redfield, the county seat of Spink county. Several railroads make the place a centre. The usual elevators are constructed at the stations. The trade of a large section of country locates itself here. Stores, banks, offices, hotels, churches, county buildings, good schools, water works, flour mills, creamery, wood-working establishment, they all serve the town and give it the pleasant appearance of prosperity. We visited many farms in the neighborhood of Redfield. As we discussed lands, harvests, investments we gained fresh knowledge concerning the matchless advancement of this country. It is one of those things that cannot be obstructed, the ultimate pre-ëminence of Dakota as the agricultural autocrat among the States. The record of bank transactions through the autumn astounds the unsophisticated New Englander. Money channels itself through these institutions with such a continuity and largeness of flow that one gets the impression that it is minted in the very fields. Eastern capital wedded to western industry yields its splendid harvest. The amount of banking business transacted by one National bank in Redfield would be creditable and noteworthy for many cities of the east.

One observes similar characteristics as Huron, Mitchell, Pierre, Madison, Chamberlain are visited. Business moves with briskness and enthusiasm. It is not speculation. Agricultural and trade sections are not favorable for speculative purposes. Values are even and reliable, with a healthful movement in the way of appreciation. People who buy land here testify unanimously to the profit of the investment, since lands are rising in value. And people who buy city property with discretion are equally secure in respect to ample profits. City real estate has doubled in price during the last two or three or five years. It is matter of necessity. South Dakota is bound to grow. Immigration besieges the Territory. The impulse of development is irresistible. Improvement, industry, expansion, settlement—they all enhance the worth of property, and contribute their share to security and stability. Huron has many substantial buildings, and considerable wealth is located in the city. Many handsome private residences give a certain home appearance to the place that commends it to the traveler. Streets are lighted by electricity, as are the streets of Aberdeen and Watertown. Water is supplied by a strong-pressure artesian well. Street railway, railroad shops, pork-packing house, flour mills, oil storage tanks, and various industrial establishments, give the city a prosperous business appearance. The schools and the churches of Huron are doing admirable work. In fact, this is characteristic of Dakota towns. One notes the same thing in Yankton. People are alert to material prosperity, yet they put strong emphasis upon school and church. Yankton has an appearance of age as compared with her city competitors. Numerous shops and public institutions give employment to a large company of men. The streets—many of them—are adorned with shade trees. One has the feeling that Yankton may be further east than some other Dakota cities. And yet age will modify the temper and appearance of all these impulsive, palpitant cities. One ought not to say one word to their disparagement. Sioux Falls is one of the liveliest towns in the West. Its trade has developed with marvelous rapidity. And it is forcible illustration of the manufacturing possibilities of the Territory. Flour mills, stove works, packing houses, wood shops, cracker factory, foundries, broom factory, bottling works, cooper shops, carriage shops, creamery, cheese factory, brick yards, cigar factories, and various other factories are all in successful operation here. The city has the telephone system, street railways, gas works, water works, electric light plant, some fourteen or fifteen churches, several educational and Territorial institutions, an opera house, fire department, and county buildings. The people themselves are thoroughly alive to the interests of the city. They propose to enlarge their enterprises, to increase their trade facilities. And their zeal will bring them rich reward. Sioux Falls will soon attain the proportions of a robust city. Men and opportunities are the two prime factors in the making of great cities. Dakota has the men—men of faith, spirit, sagacity, perseverance. Dakota has the opportunities—opportunities that history scarcely parallels. Dakota will have large cities—prosperous, opulent, well-governed, progressive. And these cities will bear close, intimate relations to the development and importance of Dakota.

STATEHOOD.

Dakota is majestic in its proportions. It spaces one hundred and fifty thousand square miles. As we cut it into acres, it takes eight figures to denote the result. Dakota gives us 96,596,480 acre lots. The landscape seems illimitable. Such vast dimensions tax the mind unto weariness. We want to think of Delaware or Connecticut for a moment, in order to rest us in our fatigue. It takes ten Denmarks to make one Dakota. We will think of little Denmark as a brief and happy respite.

The productiveness of this land matches its magnitude. The harvests seem limited only by man's capacity to till the acres and garner the increase. Wheat, rye, oats, flax, corn, barley, vegetables, flourish after a regal fashion, while flocks of sheep and herds of cattle add their precious contributions to the prosperity of the land.

These level, fertile, mighty acres invite the sovereignty of man. The rightful masters take possession. It is a large company that is distributed through Dakota. The statisticians bade us write that the round number to-day was nearly seven hundred thousand people. It is a population which exceeds the population of any other Territory. It is a population that exceeds the

E

population of Nevada, Delaware, Oregon, Colorado,
Florida, Rhode Island, Vermont, New Hampshire,
Nebraska, and probably West Virginia, Connecticut
and Maine. We may count Dakota number twenty-
two among the States and Territories, in respect to
population.

We visited these Dakota workmen. We met them
in the field, in the home, in the shop, in the store.
We traveled with them through the Territory. We
examined their schools and institutions. We went
into their churches.

We used every opportunity to study the people and
measure their worth. These people impressed us with
their manliness, their intelligence, their energy, their
thrift, their adaptability, their patriotism.

It is an Anglo-Saxon host which greets us in South
Dakota. When these young people get some infusion
of other life, it is swiftly assimilated, so that the
Anglo-Saxon spirit remains characteristic. And we
Anglo-Saxon men are great sticklers for independency,
right of representation, self-government, home rule.
Is it a strange thing, is it a presumptuous thing, that
these hundreds of thousands of educated, enterprising,
patriotic men meet in general convocation and demand
just recognition? For five years have these people
pressed their suit. Nevada, with her dwindling population of some 60,000 people, sends her representatives
to Congress. Dakota, with her more than ten times
larger population, knocks importunately at the door of

Congress, and gets a gruff answer to her appeal. The people of the Territory we found terribly in earnest concerning this important matter. It is the supreme question of the hour. They meet in frequent assembly to discuss their course of action. Tradesmen meet. The learned professions meet. Farmers, bankers meet. They agitate this question of inalienable rights. We were profoundly moved by the intensity of feeling manifested. First it is one section of the Territory, then it is another section of the Territory, then it is the whole Territory convening with this same just end in view—the achievement of Statehood. All classes chorus a great desire, urgency, passion, for Statehood. These people represent the thrift, the spirit, the manhood, the worth of New England, Pennsylvania, Ohio, New York, Indiana, and other States. These people pushed westward moved by that impulse of empire that seems native to the American heart. And the nation says to each loyal, ambitious citizen of this Territory, "Thou shalt not vote." Do these people live in the great Republic? Put that question to them when the tax-gatherer visits them. "Thou shalt not vote," says the nation, "but thou shalt pay thy taxes or be put up at auction." This is the condition in which a great host of Anglo-Saxon people, born freemen and suffragists, live and suffer and struggle.

We were quickened into sympathy with these people. They are peaceful, law-abiding citizens. They hold the interests of the Republic as most precious.

They flame with enthusiasm when national holidays remind them of great achievements. But they have a practical, personal way of interpreting their own interests. The continuance of Territorial rule signifies oppression. Public affairs are conducted after a fashion that does scant justice to various sections and industries and interests. The people have no voice in determining certain questions that pertain to their prosperity. When individuals are defrauded and when their rights are denied, we were told that any appeal to the courts was a matter of infinite patience and uncertain issue. There are six judges given to the whole Territory. Civil cases await trial year after year, so that men have learned that it was more profitable to suffer in silence than put their cause into court.

The continuance of Territorial rule signifies misgovernment. Officials are not responsible to the people. They do not represent the thought, purpose, spirit of the people. A citizen of Connecticut suddenly transferred to California would not be competent to take charge of that great State and conduct its affairs according to the will and mind of its citizens. It requires residence, observation, experience to fit men for positions of public trust. With the best intentions, men who are strangers to these Territorial conditions often make such mistakes that irreparable injury is done. That is the claim made by the citizens of Dakota—a claim that appears substantiated by their strong array of facts.

Continuance of Territorial rule signifies retardation.
The Territory is hampered. What action the local
Legislature may take is so restricted and curtailed by
national law or official veto that the citizens have small
opportunity to shape public affairs. The formative
condition of Dakota suggests many matters that require
wise deliberation and judicious adjustment. The citizens are compelled to adjourn the settlement of such
matters. They have not the power or the opportunity
to legislate for them. Any local expression of wish or
purpose is quite likely to get faint recognition when it
reaches the "powers that be." When we think how
the innumerable details of self-government are left in
this inchoate state, we are forced to confess that these
people are miserably cramped by circumstances.

The people first demand a division of the Territory.
They are very strenuous concerning this matter. Division will gain them better government. The present
capital is Bismarck. It is a long and tedious way from
Yankton, Chamberlain, the Black Hills and other parts
of the Territory. The business that is transacted at
Bismark seems quite foreign to these distant sections.
If any local matter presents itself, the people say that
they are likely to fail in getting a just hearing. Their
local interests are forgotten by the time they are transported to the distant capital. There is a certain un-
likeness between North Dakota and South Dakota
which helps to jeopard each other's interests. Legislation which favors the upper tier of counties may prove

quite harmful to the lower tier of counties, and *vice versa.* Legislation which is essential to the southeast may have no importance in the northwest. The Territory is vast, cumbrous, diversified as to interests, divided as to activities. Two States will solve the difficulty. Division is imperative.

Division will give them stronger government. The people are left to their own independent course concerning many affairs. They will find strength in cooperation. When the State takes public matters in hand, they move with the strength of the State behind them. The individual merges his share of help in the oneness of the body politic. Little opportunity then for that personal envy or opposition which is sometimes observable when public improvements and enterprises revert simply to individuals. The heartiness of general co-operation gives strength to expression of community and State life. The spirit of zealous self-help becomes universal. There is a vigor and impulse to public work that magnifies the worth of the State at the same time that it fosters and develops State power and influence.

Division will give the people a more just government. It is a wise thing for people to watch closely the men that perform public tasks. A government of the people, for the people, by the people, is the kind of government that we Americans want. Such a government has justice as one great factor. But you do not find that sort of thing in ponderous Dakota. The people want to govern themselves, and they want to do it on a scale, and after a method, suited to their condition. So they demand a North Dakota and a South Dakota. The 7th Standard parallel has already been emphasized as a division line. North of it we find the University of North Dakota, south of it the University of South Dakota. In the north is a Normal School, in the south a Normal School. In the north they locate a penitentiary, in the south they locate a penitentiary. When the north has an insane asylum then the south must have an insane asylum. Division is declared by the election of the people, by the exigencies of circumstances, by the characteristics of the two sections, by the demands of strict justice, by the events of the past fifteen years, by the laws of traffic and communication, by the organization and operation of political, educational and religious associations.

Statehood, therefore, means convenience of government to the people of Dakota. We met delegates to a Territorial Convention as we journeyed through the country. They came long distances. They made just complaint. One delegate was obliged to travel one thousand miles in order to attend this meeting. Now people in the west are not critical in respect to miles. A trip of three hundred miles or five hundred miles is a mere jaunt; but when it comes to a one thousand mile journey for the purpose of transacting a little home business, these people point to the injustice and burdensomeness of the thing. Statehood means con-

venience to South Dakota. It means an accessible
capital, a central State government, a legislative
body whose members shall hold vital communication
with their constituents. There was a time when
Rhode Island must have two capitals to accommodate
her people. Dakota, containing well nigh one hundred
and fifty times the number of acres put into Rhode
Island, must satisfy herself with one capital. The
Connecticut legislators can tarry at the capital in
Hartford until Saturday afternoon at four o'clock and
then hie themselves home to spend Sunday with their
families. Some of these Dakota legislators would be
compelled to spend the large share of every week upon
the railroad did they try to imitate the domestic ex-
ample of their Connecticut brothers. People wish to
hear their representatives make their great speeches.
People occasionally wish to see those honorable bodies
of citizens named the Assembly and the Senate. It
does the farmer, the merchant, the preacher, the la-
borer, the physician, the teacher good to come into
contact with these men who represent our intelligence,
wisdom, ability, merit. We eastern people make
periodic visits to our capitals. We observe public
proceedings with closest scrutiny. We approve or
disapprove the course that legislators take with a frank-
ness and a vigilance that insure us satisfactory legis-
tion and sound, acceptable government. Our capitals
are convenient. They are next door to our numerous
cities. And we reap great benefit from such nearness.

Now South Dakota brethren feel the necessity for just that nearness and neighborliness. They want their capital where they can visit it without making a journey of seven hundred or a thousand miles. They want their capital where they can enjoy the eloquence of their orators and observe the drift of affairs and share the spirit of great occasions without too large an expenditure of time and money. A State government centrally located serves the people. Courts adequate to the proper adjudication of causes—compe. tent, representative men who devote their time to the protection and encouragement of individual and State interests—they are a great convenience. Dakota demands such convenience.

Statehood signifies economy. When the homes of the people are near to the government, the expenses of travel are insignificant. The people hold intimate relations with their public officers and the machinery of State, and the cost of close association is comparatively small. It is a fact that two small States are governed at less expense than one large State. The same large Territory, divided into equal States, will have public affairs conducted with better economy. But the emphasis which men put upon this economic phase of the question is measured when it is observed that the people have little or nothing to say concerning taxation and expenditure. Strangers and pilgrims take these matters in hand. As their personal interests are not involved, the public money cannot have the same mean-

ing to them. The citizens of Dakota annually pay
hundreds of thousands of dollars of internal revenue ;
they pay hundreds of thousands of dollars of postage ;
and yet they are not permitted to say anything as to
the spending of these taxes. "No taxation without
representation!" Is not that the old-time cry of liber-
ty-lovers? And yet here is a host of American citizens,
almost seven hundred thousand strong, sustaining such
grievance and ignominy ! These people support various
public institutions. They support them loyally. They
never grudge their dollars. But this money is distributed by men under Federal appointment. The people cannot designate any commissioner. The public
schools of the Territory are famous. They will stamp
Dakota with their own peculiar merit. These public
schools, constantly increasing in number and expense,
representing a cost of nearly $2,000,000 for 1887,
are supported by taxes levied upon the uncomplaining
people, while millions of acres of land, assigned the
Territory for the purposes of school support, lie idle
and profitless, since the lands cannot be sold until
Dakota gets admission into the sisterhood of States.
Men can generally manage their own business better
than any neighbor. It is safe to say that States know
their own needs, and are competent to conduct their
own affairs, better than any neighbor State. Dakota
stands ready and solicitous to prove it.

Statehood signifies multiplied prosperity. We
heard it iterated and reiterated that thousands and

tens of thousands of people will make Dakota their home when Statehood is realized. There is a certain disgrace and discouragement in the present condition of things that influences many proud, ambitious people. This migration into political dependence, helplessness, disfranchisement, has features that annoy and harass the free-born, intelligent, patriotic, self-governed American citizen. A man makes a sacrifice that is something more than sentimental. It is sacrifice that means personal humiliation, political obliteration, national exile. This is thoroughly un-American and repugnant. Nevertheless, thousands of our best citizens have submitted to this sort of thing. They have submitted to it because they believed it a temporary condition. They have submitted to it because they put confidence in the national sense of justice and the national pride of spirit. But these abused, neglected men now feel that Statehood is vital to their prosperity. They alone are competent to foster and interpret State interests. They alone comprehend the issues at stake. It is time that they had the full conduct of their own affairs. There are 23,000,000 acres of public land now subject to entry. The great Sioux reservation will prove fresh and powerful stimulus to immigration. It is important that Dakota choose her public servants, and elect her local servants, in order that the great task of shaping the people into a strong, cohesive, symmetrical body politic be thoroughly and permanently and satisfactorily achieved.

Statehood will multiply prosperity. It is the testimony of business men. The State would speedily settle questions which concern the enlargement of trade. Men refuse to peril fortune in great enterprises when the laws of the land do not afford them wise protection. Certain industries have not been planted in Dakota, because capitalists found the Territorial conditions unfavorable. Men who believe that South Dakota will gain admission as a State within the next few months are making expression of such confidence by the large investment of money. The opportunities for such investments are rare and rich with promise. It just needs this one factor of State autonomy, when trade, immigration, capital, expansion will make such record as shall outstrip all recent, notable progress and give Dakota her merited eminence and power. Ireland is one-fifth the size of Dakota, and Gladstone says, "Give her home rule!" But Ireland does not easily affiliate with Great Britain, and Irish blood retains its characteristic tone and impulse. Dakota—the fair, great land—is peopled by our brothers. We are kinned by family relations, and social relations, and trade relations, and money relations, and Christian relations, and national relations. Do we need some Gladstone to traverse this Republic and say, "Give her home rule?" Nay. Dakota will submit her righteous cause to the American people.

CONCLUSION.

The Dakota days stretch themselves through many hours. We did not rise early in the morning so that we could measure their length, but we were told it was daylight a little after two o'clock. The evenings have the sun's illuminations until eight o'clock or later, and we were able to read the newspaper at half-past nine o'clock without gas or lamp. The twilights, who can forget them? They linger into the night and depart with such reluctance that we did not try to tarry upon their going. Nevertheless, the days were not long enough for us to see and to do the things which we had planned The company of friends, with all their liberal help and wise method and practical guide-work could not show us all the treasures and enterprises and institutions of South Dakota. But we gleaned wearilessly during the hurried weeks, and our loyal associates added their sheaves, so that we returned east with such harvest of facts as we present through these pages. We express hearty thanks to the Commissioner of Immigration, to various Territorial officials, to several College Presidents, to many bankers, real estate agents, merchants, farmers, railroad men, teachers, editors, laborers, commercial travelers, who gave us valuable information, and shared in showing us the land.

And now we turn us toward the future. What prophecy do we find written in the narrative of South Dakota's achievement? The railroads have just begun their unique tasks. When Dakota has the railroad facilities that serve Illinois (as have them she will), it will make 30,000 miles of iron service. The railroads are growing in all directions. One thousand miles per year is the estimate of a financier. That will soon increase. And this railroad expansion signifies the swift and thorough development of the country. Immigration is continuous and unprecedented. It disperses all through the Territory. The trains we saw doing a constant work of distribution. But the great Sioux Reservation will prove fresh and powerful stimulus to the regular and methodic plans of immigration. This Reservation, which will be opened for settlement in the autumn, containes more than 26,000,000 acres of excellent land. A part of this immense tract will speedily be subdued by the pioneer. It means an enormous influx of people. Then the east gets nearer to the west. Now that we have traversed this great interior, we observe that it is quite nigh to our seaboard markets. Railroad transportation is quick and easy. Water transportation is cheap and serviceable. The staple farm products of the west compete successfully with the farm products of the east, and the west will certainly distance her competitors. This midland section of the United States is a country that fosters all home-making. We journeyed through Kansas, Nebraska,

Iowa, Minnesota, and we were agreeably impressed with the home character of the people. Dakota, Nebraska, Kansas, they make one affluent, illimitable, productive plain. Such farm possibilities run riot with the imagination. No class of men show better judgment and keener foresight than our bankers. They pronounce with unequivocal unanimity upon the destinies of this land. In 1880 Dakota had twenty-four banks. Their capital was stated as $513,579. In 1887 the banks had multiplied into two hundred and ninty-nine, with a capital and surplus of $8,142,587. Add to this the business of fifty-one loan and mortgage companies and there is shown a capital of $11,293,981. Dakota has more banks than twenty-eight of the States. These institutions transact a business that witnesses to the thrifty, workful, enterprising character of all concerned. The investment of eastern capital in South Dakota proves very lucrative and satisfactory to the investor. "Never was the confidence of the money men of the east more solid," says Theodore Roosevelt. At the same time this money is good servant to the people in the work of improvement and expansion. As we think upon the promise and destiny of this fine portion of the Republic, we share the great assurance of the people. A prosperous, majestic commonwealth is the inevitable issue of the years. The self-denial, discomfort, struggle of land conquest will be ended, and the splendid rewards of an opulent and cultivated country may make bountiful compensation for all labor and investment.

www.ingramcontent.com/pod-product-compliance
Lightning Source LLC
Chambersburg PA
CBHW022021080426
42733CB00007B/678